Inspiration for Professional Learning Communities at Work™

A Leader's Companion

Robert Eaker
Rebecca DuFour
Richard DuFour

304 West Kirkwood Avenue
Bloomington, IN 47404
(800) 733-6786 (toll free) / (812) 336-7700
FAX: (812) 336-7790
email: info@solution-tree.com
www.solution-tree.com

Cover design by Grannan Graphic Design, Ltd.

Printed in the United States of America

ISBN 978-1-934009-05-5

Dedication

In our work with schools across North America, we have had the pleasure of meeting many outstanding educators as they have worked to transform their schools into professional learning communities. We have been impressed and encouraged by their commitment, hard work, and professionalism. A few have become close friends. This book is dedicated to them in recognition for their help, encouragement, support, and friendship.

—*Robert Eaker*
Rebecca DuFour
Richard DuFour

Other PLC Resources by the Authors

Getting Started: Reculturing Schools to Become Professional Learning Communities

Learning by Doing: A Handbook for Professional Learning Communities at Work™ (with Tom Many)

On Common Ground: The Power of Professional Learning Communities

Professional Learning Communities at Work™: Best Practices for Enhancing Student Achievement

Professional Learning Communities at Work™ Plan Book

Whatever It Takes: How Professional Learning Communities Respond When Kids Don't Learn (with Gayle Karhanek)

Contents

Preface

THE IDEA OF SCHOOLS functioning as professional learning communities strikes a positive cord with most educators. Few disagree with the notion that schools should be built on a solid foundation of collaboratively developed mission, vision, values, and goals. Few contend that schools are better served by a culture of teacher isolation rather than a collaborative culture. Few disagree with the call for schools in which educators work together to engage in collective inquiry, seek out "best practices," and implement those practices within their own classrooms, teams, and schools. And importantly, in this age of increased accountability, few oppose the premise that schools should develop a culture of continuous improvement and a focus on results—with "results" being defined as improved student learning.

In fact, never before has there been such widespread agreement about the best path to creating such schools. Researchers, practitioners, and major educational organizations have sounded the clarion call for the reculturing of schools into professional learning communities. So, the goal is clear. The challenges are straightforward: First, how do we create such schools? And second, can we demonstrate the collective will to sustain the reculturing process inherent in the PLC journey?

We remain convinced that strong, widely dispersed leadership is essential to the successful implementation of PLC concepts. Those concepts are indeed powerful, but they will not compensate for weak and ineffective leadership.

In our previous books we have attempted to help school leaders understand not only the "why" of professional learning community practices, but also the "how." A common theme present throughout our work is a call to action: "Get started, do the work."

We recognize, however, that even those who respond enthusiastically to professional learning community concepts and practices may still consider the implementation challenges to be daunting. It has been said that "even the grandest design eventually degenerates into hard work." Furthermore, the creation of a professional learning community is the result of a process rather than a prescribed program—there is no easy recipe to which one can refer for detailed, step-by-step instructions. Thus, while many educators respond to the PLC premise with initial enthusiasm, the crush of their myriad daily duties, the demands they confront on a routine basis, and the complexity of transforming a school can make it difficult to sustain that enthusiasm.

We created this book to help school leaders return their attention to the major concepts that drive the work of a PLC, recommit to those concepts, and sustain the effort needed to bring them to life in their schools. *A Leader's Companion* is a collection of the "big ideas" from each of our previous books, a quick reference to the essentials.

We hope this book will not only serve as a guide, but that it will motivate and inspire as well. Creating professional learning communities will require both passion and persistence, and it is our sincere hope this little "companion" will offer help, comfort, and inspiration to school leaders who are undertaking this important journey. We wish them Godspeed.

—Robert Eaker

Rebecca DuFour

Richard DuFour

THOSE WHO HOPE TO LEAD the process of building a PLC will return, with boorish redundancy, to the big ideas that drive the concept. Their message will be simple:

> The purpose of our school is to see to it that all our students learn at high levels, and the future of our students depends on our success. We must work collaboratively to achieve that purpose, because it is impossible to accomplish if we work in isolation. And we must continually access our effectiveness in achieving our purpose on the basis of results––tangible evidence that our students are acquiring the knowledge, skills, and dispositions we feel are essential to their future success.
>
> —*On Common Ground*

PROFESSIONAL LEARNING COMMUNITIES set out to restore and increase the passion of teachers by not only reminding them of the moral purpose of their work, but also by creating the conditions that allow them to do that work successfully.

—*Learning by Doing*

WHEN EDUCATORS LEARN to clarify their priorities, to assess the current reality of their situation, to work together, and to build continuous improvement into the very fabric of their collective work, they create conditions for the ongoing learning and self-efficacy essential to solving whatever problems they confront.

—*Learning by Doing*

THE GOAL IS NOT SIMPLY LEARNING a new system, but creating conditions for perpetual learning. It is an environment in which innovation and experimentation are not viewed as tasks to be accomplished or projects to be completed; rather they become ways of conducting day-to-day business—*forever.*

—*Whatever It Takes*

In a professional learning community educators create an environment that fosters mutual cooperation, emotional support, and personal growth as they work together to achieve what they cannot accomplish alone.

—*PLC at Work*

PLC PRINCIPLES ARE NOT JUST ARTICULATED by those in positions of leadership; even more important, they are embedded in the hearts and minds of people throughout the school.

—*PLC at Work*

E DO NOT ARGUE that the PLC journey is an easy one, but we know with certainty that it is a journey worth taking.

—*Learning by Doing*

THE FOUNDATION OF A PROFESSIONAL LEARNING COMMUNITY includes a clear sense of purpose or mission, a shared sense of vision of what we're trying to become as a school, an agreed-upon set of collective commitments or values that state the actions we will take in moving our school in the desired direction, and specific goals that serve as benchmarks to monitor our progress.

—*Getting Started*

WHAT IS OUR PURPOSE, the core reason our organization was created? What must we become as a school to better fulfill that purpose? What collective commitments must we make to move our school in the direction we want it to go? What targets and timelines are we willing to establish to serve as benchmarks of our progress?

—Getting Started

THE PROFESSIONAL LEARNING COMMUNITY model flows from the assumption that the core mission of formal education is not simply to ensure that students are taught but to ensure that they learn. This simple shift—from a focus on teaching to a focus on learning—has profound implications for schools.

—*On Common Ground*

THE TRUE MISSION OF A SCHOOL is revealed by what people do, not by what they say. Therefore, educators committed to bringing their mission statements to life in their school are relentless in examining every practice, procedure, and decision and in asking, "Is this consistent with our mission of high levels of learning for all students?"

—*On Common Ground*

HE WORDS OF A MISSION STATEMENT are not worth the paper they are written on unless people begin to do differently.

—*Learning by Doing*

UNTIL EDUCATORS CAN DESCRIBE the ideal school they are trying to create, it is impossible to develop policies, procedures, or programs that will help make that ideal a reality.

—*PLC at Work*

WHEN EDUCATORS HAVE a clear sense of the purpose, direction, and the ideal future state of their school, they are better able to understand their ongoing roles within the school.

—*PLC at Work*

MEMBERS OF A PROFESSIONAL LEARNING COMMUNITY are not content merely to describe the future they seek; they also articulate and promote the attitudes, behaviors, and collective commitments that must exist to create that future.

—PLC at Work

THE MOST EFFECTIVE STRATEGY for influencing and changing an organization's culture is simply to identify, articulate, model, promote, and protect shared values—that is, the collective commitments that will define that organization.

—*PLC at Work*

INTENTIONS ARE FINE, but they will not impact results unless and until they are translated into collective commitments and specific concrete actions.

—*On Common Ground*

RINCIPALS OF PROFESSIONAL LEARNING COMMUNITIES lead through shared vision and values rather than through rules and procedures.

—*PLC at Work*

THE CRITICAL PARAMETER, the criterion by which all behavior and decision-making in the school must be assessed, is this question: Is this action or behavior consistent with our vision and values?

—*PLC at Work*

It has often been said that an improvement process represents a journey rather than a destination, but even a journey needs ports of call along the way. Goals provide these ports of call and serve as landmarks in an improvement process.

—*PLC at Work*

A CRITICAL STEP IN MOVING AN ORGANIZATION from rhetoric to reality is to establish the indicators of progress to be monitored, the process for monitoring them, and the means of sharing results with people throughout the organization.

—*Learning by Doing*

Effective goals foster both the results orientation of a PLC and individual and collective accountability for achieving the results. They help close the gap between the current reality and where the staff hopes to take the school (the shared vision).

—*Learning by Doing*

HANGE INITIATIVES RISK LOSING MOMENTUM if there are no short-term goals to reach and celebrate.

—*PLC at Work*

STAFF WILL COME TO REGARD mission, vision, values, and goals as meaningful and important only if the principal pays attention to them on a daily basis.

—*PLC at Work*

EADERSHIP IS THE DYNAMIC that pulls together all the various elements of a professional learning community and maintains and supports them.

—*Getting Started*

Educators will remain the most important resource in the battle to provide every child with a quality education, and thus leaders must commit to creating the conditions in which those educators can continue to grow and learn as professionals.

—*Learning by Doing*

MPOWERED TEACHERS AND STRONG PRINCIPALS are not mutually exclusive goals. Schools that operate as learning communities will have both.

—*PLC at Work*

PROFESSIONAL LEARNING COMMUNITIES are guided by a culture that is simultaneously loose and tight. Leaders empower individuals and teams and encourage personal autonomy (loose) within well-defined parameters and priorities that all are expected to honor (tight).

—*PLC at Work*

HE CREATION OF A GUIDING COALITION or leadership team is a critical first step in the complex task of leading a school.

—*Learning by Doing*

GREAT TEACHERS DEMONSTRATE the qualities of great leaders—a clear sense of what must be accomplished, a gift for communication, an ability to motivate and inspire others, and a willingness to accept responsibility for results. Principals must foster this image of the teacher as a leader and demonstrate that they regard teachers as fellow leaders rather than as subordinates.

—*PLC at Work*

LEADERS OF PLCs MUST consistently communicate, through their words and actions, their conviction that the people in their school or district are capable of accomplishing great things through their collective efforts.

—*Learning by Doing*

ONE OF THE GREAT IRONIES IN EDUCATION is that it takes strong and effective educational leaders to create truly empowered people who are capable of sustaining improvement after the leader has gone.

—*Learning by Doing*

It has been said that the leaders of the past knew how to tell. The leaders of the future, however, will have to know how to ask. Those who lead the PLC process should not be expected to have all the answers and tell others what they must do. Leaders should instead be prepared to ask the right questions, facilitate the dialogue, and help build shared knowledge.

—*Learning by Doing*

TIME SPENT UP FRONT building shared knowledge results in faster, more effective, and most importantly, more committed action later in the improvement process.

—*Learning by Doing*

LEADERS SHOULD START WITH and repeatedly return to "Why?" They should create a story with a teachable point of view—a succinct explanation of the school or district's purpose and how the initiative is advancing that purpose—and they should repeat that story with boorish redundancy.

—*Learning by Doing*

WHILE LEADERS NEED A FEW KEY BIG IDEAS to provide the conceptual framework and coherence essential to successful school improvement, it is equally imperative that they recognize the need for specific, short-term implementation steps to advance those ideas.

—*Whatever It Takes*

THE LEADER'S ROLE in a professional learning community is to promote, protect, and defend the school's vision and values and to confront behavior that is inconsistent with the school's vision and values.

—*Getting Started*

LEADERS MUST SOLICIT THE IDEAS and concerns of staff. They must be willing to adapt and modify specific strategies and timelines. They must, however, remain steadfast (that is, tight) regarding the fundamental purpose and ongoing priorities of their schools.

—*Learning by Doing*

THE MOST COMMON CAUSE of the demise of PLC initiatives is not the result of a single cataclysmic event, but rather repeated compromises regarding the fundamental premises of PLCs. There is no one fatal blow: PLCs die from a thousand small wounds.

—Learning by Doing

If leaders allow participation in PLC processes to be optional, they doom the initiative to failure. . . . Substantive change that transforms a culture will ultimately require more than an invitation.

—*Learning by Doing*

IT IS POSSIBLE to be tough-minded and adamant about protecting purpose and priorities while also being tender with people.

—*Learning by Doing*

THE QUESTION SCHOOLS MUST FACE is not, "How can we eliminate all potential for conflict as we go through this process?" but rather, "How will we react when we are immersed in the conflict that accompanies significant change?"

—*Whatever It Takes*

MEMBERS OF A PROFESSIONAL LEARNING COMMUNITY view conflict as a source of creative energy and an opportunity for building shared knowledge. They create specific strategies for exploring one another's thinking, and they make a conscious effort to understand as well as to be understood.

—Learning by Doing

THE RECOGNITION that they will not be universally loved despite their best efforts may trouble leaders initially; however, once they come to accept that truth, it can be quite liberating.

—Learning by Doing

LEADERS MUST REALIZE that the most important element in communicating is congruency between their actions and their words. It is not essential that leaders are eloquent or clever; it is imperative, however, that they demonstrate consistency between what they say and what they do.

—*Learning by Doing*

EXAMPLE IS STILL the most powerful teacher. . . . If a leader resonates energy and enthusiasm, an organization thrives; if a leader spreads negativity and dissonance, it flounders.

—*Learning by Doing*

EADERS OF PROFESSIONAL LEARNING COMMUNITIES engage staff in examining what the school is being attentive to:

- What systems have we created to ensure priorities are addressed,
- What are we monitoring,
- What questions are we asking and answering together,
- What are we modeling,
- What are we celebrating,
- What are we willing to confront, and
- How are we allocating resources—time, people, and money?

—*PLC at Work*

IF A CHANGE INITIATIVE is to be sustained, the elements of that change must be embedded within the culture of the school. Unless collective inquiry, collaborative teams, an orientation toward action, and a focus on results become part of "the way we do things around here," the effort to create a professional learning community is likely to fail.

—*PLC at Work*

ONE OF THE MOST IMPORTANT CULTURAL SHIFTS that must take place if schools are to perform as professional learning communities involves a shift from a primary focus on *teaching* to placing the primary focus on *learning*.

—*Getting Started*

THE FOCUS OF TRADITIONAL SCHOOLS IS TEACHING; the focus of the professional learning community is student learning. The difference is much more than semantics. It represents a fundamental shift in the teacher-student relationship. This new relationship would not allow for the familiar teacher lament, "I taught it—they just did not learn it."

—*PLC at Work*

OU SHOULD CONSIDER THE FOLLOWING QUESTIONS if you are going to build a professional learning community in your school:

1. Does every teacher understand what each student should know and be able to do after completing the unit of instruction, course, and grade level?
2. What systems are in place to monitor each student's learning on a timely basis?
3. What happens when a student is not learning? How does the school respond?
4. What systems are in place to provide these students with additional time and support?

—*Getting Started*

WHEN A SCHOOL OR DISTRICT FUNCTIONS AS A PLC, educators within the organization embrace high levels of learning for all students as both the reason the organization exists and the fundamental responsibility of those who work within it.

—*Learning by Doing*

If the organization is to become more effective in helping all students learn, the adults in the organization must also be continually learning. Therefore, structures are created to ensure staff members engage in job-embedded learning as part of their routine work practices.

—*Learning by Doing*

SCHOOL LEADERS MUST DO MORE than deliver curriculum documents to teachers to ensure all students have an opportunity to master the same essential learning. They must engage every teacher in a collaborative process to study, to clarify, and most importantly, to commit to teaching the essential curriculum.

—*Learning by Doing*

UNTIL A SCHOOL HAS CLARIFIED what students should know and be able to do and the dispositions they should acquire as a result of schooling, its staff cannot function as a professional learning community.

—*PLC at Work*

THE CONSTANT COLLECTIVE INQUIRY into "What is it we want our students to learn?" and "How will we know when each student has learned it?" is a professional responsibility of every faculty member.

—*Learning by Doing*

HAVING A CLEAR CURRICULUM FOCUS means that teachers in a learning community not only decide together what students should be able to do, they also decide what not to teach.

—*PLC at Work*

IT IS AT THE TEAM LEVEL that teachers have the greatest opportunity for engagement, dialogue, and decision-making. When teachers have collaboratively studied the question of "What must our students learn," when they have created common formative assessments as a team to monitor student learning on a timely basis, and when they have promised each other to teach essential content and prepare students for the assessments, they have exponentially increased the likelihood that the agreed-upon curriculum will actually be taught.

—*Learning by Doing*

SSESSMENT OF A STUDENT'S WORK should provide a rich array of information on his or her progress and achievement.

—*PLC at Work*

NY ASSESSMENT PROCESS MUST BEGIN by defining what it means to succeed.

—*PLC at Work*

SCHOOLS THAT OPERATE AS professional learning communities use *formative* assessments on a frequent basis to ask, "Are the students learning and what steps must we take to address the needs of those who have not learned?"

—*Whatever It Takes*

COMMON, TEAM-DEVELOPED formative assessments are such a powerful tool in school improvement that, once again, no team of teachers should be allowed to opt out of creating them.

—*Learning by Doing*

COMMON ASSESSMENTS PROVIDE each teacher with feedback on how his or her students did in achieving an agreed-upon standard on a valid test in comparison to similar students attempting to achieve the same standard.

—*Getting Started*

IT IS IRONIC THAT SCHOOLS AND DISTRICTS often pride themselves in the fair and consistent application of rules and policies while at the same time ignoring the tremendous inequities in the opportunities students are given to learn and the criteria by which their learning is assessed.

—*Learning by Doing*

THE BEST WAY TO PROVIDE powerful feedback to teachers and to turn data into information that can improve teaching and learning is through team-developed and team-analyzed common formative assessments.

—*Learning by Doing*

PROFESSIONAL LEARNING COMMUNITIES create a systematic process of interventions to ensure students receive additional time and support for learning when they experience difficulty. The intervention process is timely and students are directed rather than invited to utilize the system of time and support.

—*Learning by Doing*

IN TRADITIONAL SCHOOLS, time is a fixed resource. The length of the school day, the number of minutes per class, and the number of days in the school year are all rigidly set. When time is up, it is time to move on. In a PLC, time is considered a critical component in learning, and the school becomes resourceful in providing additional time for students who need it. If learning is to be the constant for all students, time must become a variable.

—*Whatever It Takes*

WHEN A SCHOOL BEGINS TO FUNCTION as a professional learning community, teachers become aware of the incongruity between their commitment to ensure learning for all students and their lack of a coordinated strategy to respond when some students do not learn.

—*On Common Ground*

WHAT HAPPENS IN OUR SCHOOL when a student does not learn? We consider this question to be the fork in the road—the one question more than any other that will demonstrate a school's commitment to learning for all students and its progress on the road to becoming a PLC.

—*Whatever It Takes*

IT IS DISINGENUOUS FOR ANY SCHOOL to claim its purpose is to help all students learn at high levels and then fail to create a system of interventions to give struggling learners additional time and support for learning.

—*Learning by Doing*

THE KEY QUESTION THE STAFF of any school must consider in assessing the appropriateness and effectiveness of their daily schedule is, "Does the schedule provide access to students who need additional time and support during the school day in a way that does not require them to miss new direct instruction?"

—*Learning by Doing*

SYSTEMS OF INTERVENTION WORK most effectively when they are supporting teams rather then individual teachers.

—*Learning by Doing*

WE CONTEND THAT A SCHOOL truly committed to the concept of learning for each student will stop subjecting students to a haphazard, random, *de facto* educational lottery program when they struggle academically. It will stop leaving the critical question, "How will we respond when a student is not learning?" to the discretion of each teacher.

—*Whatever It Takes*

A SCHOOL WITH A MULTI-STEP SYSTEM of interventions arms itself with a variety of tools for meeting the needs of its students and thus is more likely to find the appropriate strategy.

—*Whatever It Takes*

WHEN A SCHOOL HAS DEVELOPED a system of interventions, the goal is to provide the services only until students demonstrate they are ready to assume greater responsibility for their learning. The focus is on gradually weaning the student from the extra time and support as the student becomes successful in classes. The interventions then serve as a safety net if the student should falter, but they are not intended to be a permanent crutch.

—*Whatever It Takes*

EALIZE THAT NO SUPPORT SYSTEM will compensate for bad teaching.

—*Learning by Doing*

SCHOOLS THAT FUNCTION as professional learning communities are *always* characterized by a collaborative culture. Teacher isolation is replaced with collaborative processes that are deeply embedded into the daily life of the school. Members of a PLC are not "invited" to work with colleagues: They are called upon to be contributing members of a collective effort to improve the school's capacity to help all students learn at high levels.

—*Getting Started*

THE COLLABORATIVE TEAM IS THE ENGINE that drives the PLC effort. Some organizations base their improvement strategies on efforts to enhance the knowledge and skills of individuals. Although individual growth is essential for organizational growth to take place, it does not guarantee organizational growth. Building a school's capacity to learn is a collective rather than an individual task.

—*Whatever It Takes*

THE CULTURE of a professional learning community is characterized by collaborative teams whose members work interdependently to achieve common goals, for which each member is mutually accountable. Special attention must be paid to the "interdependence" and "common goals" if we are going to have high-quality collaboration and truly effective teams.

—*Getting Started*

THE CHALLENGE FACING LEADERS is not creating the teams, but rather is providing the focus, time, support, and parameters critical to effective teamwork.

—*Getting Started*

USE THE TEAM STRUCTURE to foster a collaborative culture in your school. Be certain that the members of each team are working interdependently to achieve common goals for which they are mutually accountable, and provide each team with the parameters, resources, and information essential to its effectiveness.

—*Getting Started*

IT IS FUNDAMENTALLY UNFAIR to teachers to insist that collaboration is a priority and then fail to provide them with time to collaborate during the school day.

—*Getting Started*

In a PLC, *collaboration* represents a *systematic* process in which teachers work together interdependently in order to *impact* their classroom practice in ways that will lead to better results for their students, for their team, and for their school.

—*Learning by Doing*

It is crucial not to overlook the significance of teams developing explicit norms to guide their work in the process of building the capacity of teachers to work together collaboratively. Norms can help clarify expectations, promote open dialogue, and serve as a powerful tool for holding members accountable.

—*Learning by Doing*

In short, there is nothing more important in determining the effectiveness of a team than each member's understanding of and commitment to the achievement of results-oriented goals to which the group holds itself mutually accountable.

—*Learning by Doing*

When teachers clarify essential outcomes, develop common assessments, and set standards they want all students to achieve by test and by subtest, they are in a position to establish goals that can only be achieved if each member contributes. They can begin to function as an effective team, and effective teams are essential to the collaborative culture of a learning community.

—*Getting Started*

UNTIL THE CONCEPTUAL MODEL that guides the professional development of the staff becomes teams of teachers working together in the context of their school to develop the knowledge and skills necessary to achieve their team and school goals, that school will have difficulty becoming a PLC.

—*On Common Ground*

WHEN TEAMS BECOME THE FOCUS of celebration and every team feels it too has the opportunity to be recognized and applauded, schools begin to move away from a culture of internal competition and toward a sharing culture.

—*On Common Ground*

Collaborative Teams

COLLABORATION BY INVITATION Does Not Work!

—*PLC at Work*

MEMBERS OF PLCs ENGAGE IN *collective* inquiry: They learn how to learn together. But it is only when they focus this collective inquiry on the right questions that they develop their capacity to improve student and adult learning.

—*Learning by Doing*

THE ENGINE OF IMPROVEMENT, growth, and renewal in a professional learning community is collective inquiry. People in such a community are relentless in questioning the status quo, seeking new methods, testing those methods, and then reflecting on the results.

—*PLC at Work*

HE VERY REASON THAT TEACHERS work together in teams and engage in collective inquiry is to serve as catalysts for action.

—*Learning by Doing*

EMBERS OF PLCs ARE ACTION ORIENTED: They move quickly to turn aspirations into action and visions into reality.

—*Learning by Doing*

Wishful thinking and good intentions do not improve schools. Even serious reflection and meaningful dialogue impact school improvement only to the extent that those within the school are persuaded to act differently.

—*Getting Started*

AT THE SAME TIME LEADERS OF THE PROCESS are championing the big ideas of a PLC, they must break down the school's journey into a series of small, incremental steps that goad people to action.

—*On Common Ground*

INHERENT TO A PLC are a persistent disquiet with the status quo and a constant search for a better way to achieve goals and accomplish the purpose of the organization.

—*Learning by Doing*

TIMELY FEEDBACK IS A CRITICAL ELEMENT in any process to promote continuous improvement and ongoing learning. Individuals and teams must have access to the data and information that enable them to make adjustments as they are engaged in their work, rather than when it is completed.

—Learning by Doing

CULTURE OF CONTINUOUS IMPROVEMENT does not require a persistent state of panic.

—*PLC at Work*

MEMBERS OF A PROFESSIONAL LEARNING COMMUNITY continually assess their effectiveness on the basis of results: tangible evidence their students are acquiring the knowledge, skills, and dispositions essential to their future success.

—*Learning by Doing*

ONE OF THE MOST SIGNIFICANT TOOLS available to a school that is attempting to build a PLC is this process of clarifying essential outcomes, building common assessments, reaching consensus on the criteria by which teachers will judge the quality of student work, and working together to analyze data and improve results.

—*On Common Ground*

IN A PROFESSIONAL LEARNING COMMUNITY, educators are hungry for evidence of student learning. Relevant, timely information is the essential fuel of their continuous improvement process.

—*Learning by Doing*

UNLESS INITIATIVES ARE SUBJECTED to ongoing assessment on the basis of tangible results, they represent random groping in the dark rather than purposeful improvement.

—*Learning by Doing*

THE PROCESS OF BECOMING A PLC is designed to achieve a very specific purpose: to continuously improve the collective capacity of a group to achieve intended results. Therefore, it is incongruous to engage in elements of the process and ignore results.

—*Learning by Doing*

THE OLD ADAGE, "PRACTICE MAKES PERFECT," is patently false. Those who continue to engage in ineffective practices are unable to improve, much less reach perfection. Therefore, all practices must be examined in terms of their impact on the desired results.

—*Learning by Doing*

IF SCHOOLS ARE TO IMPROVE, they need educators who believe in the possibility of a better future—and in themselves.

—*PLC at Work*

THE CONCEPT OF HIGH EXPECTATIONS rests upon neither unwarranted optimism nor additional unsupported demands on students. It is not the perception of a staff regarding the ability of their *students* that is paramount in creating a culture of high expectations. The staff members' perceptions of their *own personal and collective ability* to help all students learn is far more critical.

—*Whatever It Takes*

A SCHOOL DOES NOT BECOME a learning community simply by advancing through the steps on a checklist, but rather by tapping into the wellsprings of emotions that lie within the professionals of that school. The professional learning community makes a conscious effort to bring those emotions to the surface and to express explicitly what often is left unsaid.

—*PLC at Work*

WE SHOULD INDEED PROMOTE HIGH LEVELS of learning for every child entrusted to us, not because of legislation or fear of sanctions, but because we have a moral and ethical imperative to do so.

—*Whatever It Takes*

Leaders provide constant reminders of the impact teachers and teams are having on the lives of students. They make heroes of staff members by weaving a never-ending story of committed people who touch both the minds and hearts of their students.

—*Learning by Doing*

CREATING A PROFESSIONAL LEARNING COMMUNITY is analogous to a "voyage," and educators must prepare themselves to be buffeted by occasional ill winds along the way. While some schools are content to lie at anchor and accept things as they are and other schools simply drift from fad to fad, the members of a professional learning community will stay the course.

—*PLC at Work*

ONE OF THE MOST IMPORTANT and effective strategies for shaping the culture of any organization is celebration. The celebrations, ceremonies, and rituals of an organization reveal a great deal about its culture—how its people link their past with their present, what behaviors are reinforced, what assumptions are at work, and what is valued.

—*PLC at Work*

WHEN AN ORGANIZATION makes a concerted effort to call attention to and celebrate progress toward its goals, the commitments it demonstrates in day-to-day work, and evidence of improved results, people within the organization are continually reminded of the priorities and what it takes to achieve them.

—*Learning by Doing*

FREQUENT PUBLIC ACKNOWLEDGEMENTS for a job well done and a wide distribution of small symbolic gestures of appreciation and admiration are far more powerful tools for communicating priorities than infrequent "grand prizes" that create a few winners and many losers.

—*Learning by Doing*

CELEBRATION WILL NOT HAVE A SIGNIFICANT EFFECT on the culture of a school if most people in the organization feel they have no opportunity to be recognized.

—*Learning by Doing*

RECOGNIZING EXTRAORDINARY COMMITMENT should be the responsibility of everyone in the organization, and each individual should be called upon to contribute to the effort.

—*Learning by Doing*

ACKNOWLEDGING, HONORING, and thanking everyone who contributes to the building of a learning community increases the likelihood that the effort will be sustained.

—*PLC at Work*

THE QUESTION CONFRONTING MOST SCHOOLS and districts is not, "What do we need to know in order to improve?" but rather, "Will we turn what we already know into action?"

—*Learning by Doing*

Here is the brutal fact: The most common reason for failure to close the knowing-doing gap is not conflict with others, but conflict from within. We fail to do what we recognize we should do simply because it is easier to continue an unquestionably ineffective or bad practice than it is to adopt a new one.

—*Learning by Doing*

ADVANCED PLC TRAINING does not come from formal training: It comes from doing the work of PLCs. It comes from trying a lot of things, learning from what works and what does not, thinking about what was learned, making adjustments, and trying again.

—*On Common Ground*

SCHOOLS THAT WAIT FOR EVERYONE to get on board the school improvement train are unlikely to ever leave the station.

—*Getting Started*

ISN'T IT IRONIC HOW FREQUENTLY we question the willingness of others to do what must be done to improve our schools, and in doing so, absolve ourselves of the responsibility for taking action?

—*Getting Started*

SCHOOLS THAT TAKE THE PLUNGE and actually begin *doing* the work of a PLC develop their capacity to help all students learn at high levels far more effectively than schools that spend years *preparing* to become PLCs through reading or even training.

—*Learning by Doing*

ACHIEVING AGREEMENT about what we are prepared to start doing, and the *implementation* of that agreement, is one of the most effective strategies for closing the knowing-doing gap. Those who "do" develop deeper knowledge, greater self-efficacy, and a stronger sense of ownership in results than those who talk about what should be done.

—*Learning by Doing*

PUBLIC EDUCATION stands at an important crossroads. At no time in our history have we, as a profession, possessed a clearer sense of what it takes to help all students learn at high levels. The question remains: Will we demonstrate the discipline and tenacity to act on that knowledge?

—*On Common Ground*

WILL EDUCATORS RECOMMIT to their fundamental mission—to ensure high levels of learning for each student? Will they pronounce that "Failure is not an option," and mean it? Will they build shared knowledge and come to a deeper understanding of their craft? Will they work together collaboratively to address their problems and challenges because they know there is no hope of success if they work in isolation? Will they recognize that in a very real sense, lives are hanging in the balance? We urge them to do so, not for the sake of improved test scores, but for the sake of the dreams and aspirations of the children whose lives they touch.

—*Whatever It Takes*

www.solution-tree.com

www.allthingsplc.info